IF ONLY THERE WERE STATIONS OF THE AIR

IF ONLY THERE WERE STATIONS OF THE AIR

POEMS

Judy Kronenfeld

Sheila-Na-Gig Editions

If Only There Were Stations of the Air © 2024 Judy Kronenfeld

Cover photo: Ruth Bavetta
The author extends her appreciation to Ms. Bavetta for this use.

Author photo: Alexis Rhone Francher

ISBN: 978-1-962405-01-0
Library of Congress Control Number: 2024935386

Sheila-Na-Gig Editions
Russell, KY
Hayley Mitchell Haugen, Editor
www.sheilanagigblog.com

For David again, and always

ACKNOWLEDGMENTS

My appreciation goes out to the past and present members of my poetry group (Ruth Bavetta, Lavina Blossom, Charlotte Davidson, Penelope Moffet, Elizabeth Morrison-Banks, and Cati Porter) for their friendship and for their lively and useful conversations about poetry, and about a good number of these poems. And, as always, my deep gratitude to my husband, David Kronenfeld, for his love, confidence, and support—especially in difficult times.

Grateful acknowledgment is made to the publications in which the following poems originally appeared, sometimes in earlier versions and occasionally with different titles:

Avatar Review: "Summer of Catastrophe"
Blue Heron Review: "Talking to Myself as I Face Surgery in the Time of Covid"
Cider Press Review: "Deep Travel"
Gyroscope Review: "Grace," "I Don't Think We Live in California," "If I Could Use the Wind Phone"
The Journal of Radical Wonder: "Cosmoses"
Juniper: "3 A.M."
MacQueen's Quinterly: "Animal Knowledge," "The Day Before My Swiftly-Scheduled Back-to-Back MRIs, I Think of Mother and Her Houseplants," "Final Dissolve by Aquamation," "Naked vs Nude"
Misfit Magazine: "Incommensurate"
Months to Years: "8th and 9th Decade"
Muddy River Poetry Review: "Coming Soon," "Green," "Strange"
North of Oxford: "Flowers Growing in Time-Lapse to Music"
Offcourse: "After, and Before," "Anticipation," "Broken Communion," "The Dead," "Escape," "Fog and Glare," "History of the *Chewy* to the Present, Plagued Moment," "I Get News of Your Death, Cousin, Four Decades after You Disappear," "Leaving," "Presence," "Theft," "Who Will Be with Them?"
One Art: "Sometimes there's no freedom to love the world—"
One Sentence Poems: "Together"
Peacock Journal: "Touch"
The Plague Papers, a special issue of *Poemeleon:* "Madame Monet and Her Son *en Plein Air*"

Right Hand Pointing: "Bodily Pain," "My Widowed Friend: Desperate to Mute the Hospital Chaplain" (originally published as "Desperate to Mute the Hospital Chaplain"), "The Old Story Never Loses Its Capacity to Shock," "The Words of Poems"

Schuylkill Valley Journal: "Hope Because"

Sheila-Na-Gig: "Afternoon, Evening, Night," "Explosion"

Verdad: "Pandemic Glissade"

Verse Virtual: "Showstopper"

CONTENTS

I

Flowers Growing in Time-Lapse to Music

In this spring of contagion, I get caught
by those videos of the vegetable world—
with its own inexorable will—
pushing up through heavy loam:
bent buds straightening
and unfolding
on stiffening stalks—
dear as cramped bird heads
stretching out
of beak-cracked eggs;
just-new petals
flutter-testing themselves—
touching as birth-wet calves
stumbling up on shaky legs.
And no decay.

All the blind plants busy
as an orchestra playing
prestissimo, almost fast enough
for my mortal eye to imagine
cotyledon to stunning blossom
known all-at-once
in timeless Mind—the barrier
of becoming, broken.
As if there were
an instant plan
for everything natural,
and it was perfectly
beneficent.

Showstopper

Did we need to be
reminded how temporary we are,
how the earth's just another
planet revolving around a star—
quickened with the accident
of life, but not forever—
how the universe itself
that somehow blinked on,
might blink off?

And reminded by you, the new crown
of viruses, taking center stage
like an egotist at a party,
monopolizing all the frequencies
(always *me me me*),
who won't let anyone else speak
about anything?

Like a ferocious wind,
you seize my words
as I open my mouth,
scatter my pink-snow-drift bloom
of poems, swallow and crush
my elegies trying to limn
the essence of someone
I loved, and mourn
an ordinary death.

Madame Monet and Her Son *en Plein Air*

(Monet's *Woman with a Parasol*, 1875)

They've just stopped their stroll this moment
and are looking down the hill she's climbed
from the other side and her son is cresting—as if
the artist below were snapping a candid photo.
This glorious day won't pause
for a formal portrait. It's all flash
and glint, air and motion, and she's
in the quicksilver of it, the details
of her shadowed face not important—
only that her veil—captured with the same
fleet brushstrokes—blows as breezily about it
as the cirrus clouds blow in the sky,
only that her scarf flutters at her neck,
her skirts swirl like rivulets of water
flowing around a rock in a stream,
her hems lift and sway as she walks.
The prism of light breaks and spills
its radiance. No color is singular:
the white of her costume
purpled and blued, and glowing yellow
on her sleeve—the wildflowers' hue
flown upward—and even her deep shadow
in the grass hints lavender and violet.
Her muted back-lit figure, and her little son's,
her parasol, intense dark green,
all heighten the light that floods the unshaded
flower-dappled grasses, and pours
and dazzles in the cloud-bright sky;
they make light's tincture
that much more tender where it daubs
the boy's shoulders and the crown
of his straw hat, pearls
the sun-streamed edge
of his mother's skirts and jacket.

Moving stillness! Stuck in our sequestered
static spaces thick with human smells,
shadowed hearts curled inwards,
we dream of airing ourselves for hours—
our bodies refreshed as wash on the line,
wind beating against us, lavish sun
spilling over our upturned faces.

3 A.M.

I wake from the cavern
of sleep on a summer night
and move in the fur of dark
towards a drink of water,
surprised by four repeated
bird-notes, a bit like Beethoven's
Fifth sped up—somewhere outside
my open window as I drain my cup—
riding the dark,
piercing it like tiny, busy,
unseen sewing machine needles.
A very learned mockingbird,
perhaps, sending out
his lonely voice long
before dawn—when there are
even fewer rival sounds
than during these deserted days—
awake with me, whistling
and trilling now, comforting,
as I lay my head
on my pillow again.

History of the *Chewy* to the Present, Plagued Moment

Our son, at two, bestowed its special name,
but it began as a clean cloth diaper
flung over my shoulder, when he was an infant,
to keep wet gurgles and spit-up
from my clothes, as I burped him
after nursing. I would lift him from me
to lay him down softly in his bassinet,
and he'd come away clutching the diaper
in his fists; soon one, or a smaller
substitute was required to gentle the night
for rest. In spite of the moniker he gave it,
he never chewed it so much
as cherished it with fingers or cheek.

To my surprise, I recognized a version,
on a long-ago visit to his grad school digs—
a piece of ancient yellow tee shirt,
already mellowed by first grade,
poking out from under his mattress.

Now he's middle-aged, at home
on another continent. We haven't seen him
for two years. We've hardly seen
anyone.

These days, his dad and I find ourselves holding
the little pillows filled with beads—
bought for our arthritic necks—
like small white pets against
our chests, until we fall asleep.

Pandemic Glissade

Lord, what am I doing
compelled into the kitchen yet again
for these milky morsels that melt me
wave on wave—punctuating my days
with velvet glosses on my tongue,
telling my hours with this recompense
until my teeth begin
to ache?—who am I kidding,
minutes, maybe, even seconds,
before the next fistful
of chocolate chips. Which hardly taste
like *chips*. Better to steal
the name of kisses, a fat-cheeked
baby's with pursed lips, each droplet
with its little silky topknot,
like the one curl on the baby's
forehead. Dark pearls drizzling
into my open mouth, upping the ante
for simple sweetness, sweepstakes sweetness,
come snow me in with flurries
of ellipses, until my ticking house
is muffled in your drifts,
and my hollow tooth feels satisfied
for years.

My Widowed Friend: Desperate to Mute the Hospital Chaplain

God gives us only as much
as we can bear he intones,
as if his leaden hands were on
my family's shoulders,
and he was breathing out on us
that peppermint-greased tautology
through his brilliantly bleached teeth. What can
be *more?* As if we're bearing it
because we're here
inside the unbearable
that has borne us
to this Zoom meeting, bears down on us
and bears no fruit
but steady tears—like useless work
we've still to do.

I Get News of Your Death, Cousin,
Four Decades after You Disappear

And I remember your Dad, rumored violent, who smiled
and smiled and smelled of too-sweet cologne,
your co-dependent Mom, suspiciously
bruised, who loved you so fiercely
she kept you weak, and always chose appearances
over the truth. And heart and mind-damaged
beautiful you, left helpless and alone
after their deaths, then driving away help
with your mad phone rants.
And I think of when we were girls,
and our families used to meet,
how each hand tried to climb the other's tree
as you snuggled your fists under your chin—
your scribbling fingers caged hamsters turning
their exercise wheels, your own little player piano
shivering a happy tune. Such a chill of pleasure
to await your uncle's and aunt's embraces!
You were like a blue-lipped child
just summoned from the sea,
shaking deliciously as she pictures
being wrapped in fleece.

A nurse said you died alone,
an old woman in a facility for adults,
after sixteen friendless years. How little
a life can be. At a time when lonely death
is legion, and could be anyone's—
whether loved by a host of friends and kin,
or last in the family line—
I record your Yahrzeit in my book,
and try to think of you at peace—
no naked wolf bearing down
on the fold, no waves of rage,
no heart like sea-crushed shells.

Fog and Glare

Brain buzzing every minute of the night,
turn left? turn right?
stay straight? I cannot reconstruct
my destination—in my dreamed mind only
raspy fog sticking like burrs, and no dissolve
into the goal I must recall, supermarket?
post office? doctor's? in order not
to be immobilized at this flashing
stoplight. Then I force my foot
off the brake to turn this closest corner
staring at me in stupor,
and then I'm wildly cornering like a bumper
car, the quiet skin of the familiar
peeled off all the buildings—
which I can neither recognize
nor ignore—revealing a stark whiteness,
mica-bright, that drills my eyes. My head on fire,
I desert the ticking van, stumbling
from the impenetrable street
through an open door. It's *Rite-Aid,*
Open Late. And like my dead, demented father,
I hand the clerk the note I carry
with the ciphers of my name and number,
hoping he can tell me who I am.

Summer of Catastrophe

Homes so cozy the walledness of them, the roofedness, creating inside, creating privacy, creating spaces to express our personalities, creating color schemes, creating places to dust, creating finds from our pasts, discoveries for our children to make. Dwellings that envelop us, separating us from the universe, helping us window-scan the not-us, situating sky, clouds, streets, trees, lawns, people . . .

We could try looking at them as if from outer space. Or, at least as though in some future history: walls cracked like eggs and devoured by 500 year Godzilla floods, sliding downstream, buried in mud, churned up, earthquaked, blown apart by hurricanes, felled like mountains of trees by erupting volcanoes, burnt down to chimney bricks.

But we can't even decide what we'd grab from the hypothetical list that never actualizes into a suitcase by the door because that suitcase would invite disaster, and—filled with doppelgangers—flummox our routines, mushrooming until it burst its seams. And because what we really want to take is the flush of morning sun on our bedroom walls, evening lamplight gentled over our books at the center of the surrounding dark, headlights wheeling over our ceilings.

We know, if given minutes, we'd run from room to room blubbering with indecision. *Our papers in the stumble-heavy fire box—or would it outlast the present catastrophe? these boots good for walking on glass or lava or ash? the three shelves of photo scrapbooks, or the external hard drives we never finished putting the photos on? flash drives? or the whole PC?*

When we're quiet dust in urns at the back of their closets, awaiting scattering, our far-away, too busy children will pay for the clearance agent to disappear all the contents of our houses—selling what can be sold, trashing diaries, photographs, most of the old books. But Nature, more thorough, and angry at us, could take the whole house, and the division, and the town, smashing to atoms our lovely illusory solidity— while we still live.

Leaving

If fire raged at the other end
of my street, and I had to escape,
I would object
But my desk is a mess—
Honestly, I need to Marie Kondo
the whole house, to find
what to take.

In the midst of war, I would speak up
like that old woman in Bakhmut
who resisted her rescuer's *Let's go!*
with *I need to pack grapes, and maybe*
some sort of pancakes,
because even an apartment
with no heat in a building blasted
by a bomb pulses like a neutron star
HOME HOME HOME.

When the Angel of Death arrives
at my door with Lethe-by-IV
for my pain, my brain will obsess—
But I haven't decided yet
whether to leave my diaries to the kids,
or burn them. And there are dishes
festering in the sink. And we're going
next week with our best friends
to that new French rest—

II

Grace

Icy, sharp-edged morning—
the shattering bark
of unseen dogs sends
sudden birds flapping away
in fast bursts.
Almost swifter than my eye,
one throttles back—engines
at a dampened thrum—
near the leafless plum
outside my study window,
and floats
to the close branch,
delicately touching down
with a grace I envy,
as my mind tries to flee
"suspicious" on a CT scan—
which could shatter me.

Coming Soon

Coming Soon: Crypts, Niches & Graves
the cemetery sign shouts as I drive past
on my way home from the hospital
where I've seen the cardio-thoracic surgeon,
alone, because they said they wouldn't let you in
as Covid surges. And did that sign actually add
an exclamation point? What step-right-up seller's
chutzpah! Or is the point implicit
in the all too literal "coming soon"? My brain
is noodling *nodule (= lesion? = tumor?),*
the "incidental finding" on a CT
previously addressing something minor.

Is it too soon to spill my limbo
of raw fear to family and friends
and risk having to swallow everything back—
ashamed and never again to be believed?
Or is the wolf not "coming soon,"
but frothing at the door, as the surgeon,
inclined to diagnose with scalpel,
seemed to imply, though unwilling
to give odds—malign or benign?

I want the lyre, or glittering bough
for a trial-run underground, return trip
guaranteed. Having brushed against
the shades, mere wisps
wafting through the vast, icy, unlit
corridors, perhaps I'd emerge more acclimated
to being dust.

I need a primer on the lonely hospital bed,
and how to endure sentience there,
a lesson in the blank stare
of the clock, its perpetually stuttering

hands. I need a guide to a body remote
as an outpost taken over by strangers,
a model of a soul without
the mute animal comfort
of touch.

I need these still when I'm at our door
with this foreign thing in my chest,
though seeing my uneasy face,
you open your warm human arms.

After, and Before

Yesterday, the flash supernova
of the likely diagnosis
almost stifled in my husband's arms,
I did want, I didn't want
the moment he gravely said,
you know I'm here
no matter what—

How much I needed
to push him away,
or have him abscond with me
into Before, how lucky I am, in After,
to have him—

though imprisoned in the citadel
of my own skin.

Today, a pre-arranged visitor muffling
the humming silence, the As If of Before
so close . . .

Yet, in the 6 a.m. supermarket
before the guest arrived, the insuperable
beauty of the Muzak—wave
upon wave of "Autumn Leaves"
flooding my ears—proof I have entered
After.

Now, at three in the morning,
I wake flailing,
pitched into a boundless sea—
fear like water
filling my mouth.

Now, it is absolute After,
and my husband sleeps
on the warm, private beach
of the well.

The Words of Poems

I think the words of poems
in the wan milk light
of dawn, when, anxious,
I awake. Frost,
Shakespeare, Yeats.
Though nothing gold
can stay, and an old woman
is a paltry thing, and I weep
to have what I fear
to lose, my lips move
in my mind till these human voices
lull me, and I sleep.

Hope Because

the gold stillness of late California afternoons,
the stillness that is like Spirit
pulling in its breath for a moment, the breath
it breathed into us and could breathe again—
that expectant—pours like slow oil
over your head too,

because you are still walking the tightrope
of your life in delicate shoes,
though the net below (is there a net?)
is invisible, and balance
is a miracle,

because light still grows in you
and might emerge in startling
bursts, like sizzles and flashes
from the farthest stars,

because your heart and mind are populated
by all the dead you keep an altar for,
the dead you visit in the reaches of dreams,
and you have your vigils mapped
for years.

Presence

This afternoon, late, as I start out
on my walk, the air feels steely
and sharp, but I
am warm in fleece and down
as spectacular light spills
over the brown mountains ahead
making them glow red
against the tenderest blue. It is a light
that says let this rising moon,
glitter-white and frost-gray,
a perfect disk of cold engraved
platinum—its features so distinct—
burn into your brain. It says
winter, still, but you can mark
the days' slow lengthening
toward spring. It says
drink this! before you arrive
at the worn path to your door,
the hills flat again, lackluster,
before you give yourself,
early tomorrow morning,
into the surgeon's strict hands.

Talking to Myself as I Face Surgery in the Time of Covid

When I awake, here, in the mansions
of the living air, not yet having had to stoop
under that lowest marble roof in that crowded
neighborhood of relentless views,
maybe even the rude stranger, pain,
will be welcome proof that I still am.
And if, when my eyelids flutter open,
I'm shaky outside the stanchions
of the beloved everyday, if I'm estranged a little
from my tube-drained chest,
let me remember how the wiry fingers
clenched tight at my sides once smoothed
the silken crowns of anxious children,
and stroked the warm bald dome
of a confused and frightened father.
Let me hold my own hands
gently in my heart—as mothers clasp
the tiny, perfect fists of newborns.

Naked vs. Nude

Naked under my sheets and paper gown, I arrive
on a gurney, and, on the count of three, am brought
to the hard narrow pallet beyond hesitation,
surrounded by masked attendees entirely swathed
in green. Their eyes below their headlights,
behind their face shields, make no contact.

The unannounced relaxant has already begun
to induce surrender, yet buried within me,
there's a radiating scream—like the one
in Edvard Munch's painting.
But my lips remain compressed
by the rules of patient decorum.

Gown and sheets will be stripped, replaced
by new sterile draping baring the site of interest,
when I—unwarned—have blinked out of consciousness.
My inert body will be briefly exposed, then
my newly draped one will reveal my chest,
as the bodies around me, sheathed to the teeth,
bend to their tasks.

What I would give not to need to be here!
Oh, to be transmuted! Even into that nude female
seated near the *brioche* and *cerises*
in Édouard Manet's *Déjeuner sur L'Herbe*—
cast in a man's dream of dapper
clothed men and disrobed women,
yet quite removed and utterly at ease,
smiling her faintly daring smile
at viewers, her power still hers.

Together

You share my room
three nights in the surgical ward,
sleeping awkwardly
on a foldout chair, as I doze
in my opiate-quieted bed—
the soothing arm's reach
between us all the sweetness
we can know.

Animal Knowledge

When I open the window blinds
above the couch my small dog lies on,
on her side, she lifts her two free legs
as automatically as Pavlov's dogs
responded to the bell. I turn to leave,
the legs drift down. I come back to water
a plant on the nearby bookcase,
they're up again. And this time,
though I'm busy, I sit
to stroke her soft, warm belly.

How good it might be, to be a pet dog.
No hunting required. No predators
to flee. No consciousness of my own
death. Just the endless succession
of moments in the present—when I'm not
asleep. The briefest tensions:
when, doing my job, I bark
at strangers passing in the street,
or wait for a tidbit of something
good—*Is that, is that, is that*
for me? No brooding that my cancer
removed last year could easily recur.
No fear that the side effects
of the ongoing treatment will shock me
again.

Then I remember my decrepit
last dog—demented, incontinent,
in pain—trying vainly to rise after the vet
injected the relaxant just before he put her
down: how she looked at me mutely
with her beseeching eyes while I wept
enough to soak my shirt—and how
that present moment swelled to fill
the universe.

The Day before My Swiftly-Scheduled Back-to-Back MRIs, I Think of Mother and Her Houseplants

Snipping a straggly stem from one of my kitchen plants
this morning, I flash on my mother diligently
wiping the dust off every philodendron leaf,
watering, feeding, pruning, then propagating or potting
more greenery for her four rooms. She was never
delicate with her hands; when I was a kid, she used
to tear the tops off cereal and baking soda boxes,
rather than master the instructions. Yet,
in her old age, her houseplants were lustrous,
bushy, thriving.

Two decades after her death, one of her clones
hangs on in my North-facing nursery window,
its leaves pale, almost translucent, needing
something—light? more light?

Right now, I miss her green too-busy nearness
feeding and shaping me, pushing my hair
from my forehead, tucking it behind my ears,
blessing the top of my head with her stroking
palm at any odd moment, trying too hard
to appease my fears. Tomorrow, the slow slide
of my immobile body into the lonely tube
of the MRI. And no-one waiting, as if the news
to come—joyous or dreadful—were her own.

Sometimes there's no freedom to love the world—

its slants of light,
its glancingness
requiring quick
open arms.

The sorrows of the body
hood your eyes.

Time places its heavy
stones steadily around
you—building, building—
until there is only
a small spot left
for your body
to curl into itself,
its own prisoner
in its cold hovel

where it dreams
of galloping through the dark
like a hero in a ballad,
drinking in the flash
and glint of dawn.

III

Who Will Be with Them?

The shadows in their rooms
slip down the walls—like flags
down masts—their windows'
light is soon to be effaced,
their balance on the earth
is fraught, their fingernails,
neglected, packed with dirt.

Let human angels hover near
the few who suddenly, stubbornly,
jettison their walkers—coveting
a dream of upright dignity—
and delicately right them,
linking arms on either side,
before they fall, yards from
the dining room.

Let some surrender wholly
to the pleasure of food, as though
they were first discovering it—
almost swooning at the succulence
of butter-dripping shrimp cut
and fed in manageable bits,
closing their eyes as they lick
raspberry sorbet from a proffered spoon.

And when the window's light is nearly
swept away, as if by the speeding
hour hand of a greedy clock,
may someone they love sit close to each
of them, cradling their bony fingers,
and whisper how important
their lives have been.

Broken Communion

We haven't really spoken for a year.
Thinking of that I feel oddly dispossessed,
like those Paris bridges quite suddenly stripped
of tens of tons of engraved padlocks—
standing in for steadfast attachments (keys tossed
into the Seine)—that threatened the collapse
of the structures they hung on.

Friendship, like love, can crest, then flail,
then fail. For forty years, we were locked
by the accidents of common circumstance.
For twenty-five years or more, our posse
of kids hung out together like siblings,
for almost forty, our husbands shot
the workday breeze, our calendars were dotted
with joint dinners, campouts, holidays, trips.

Is there an inventory somewhere of the confidences
that poured from us, fueled—before we quit—
by cigarettes and brandy? My heart spilled out
in conversation, lost its melancholy, was refreshed
as spring-cleaned rooms, thoroughly dusted, swept,
scrubbed, aired.

Gradually, our weaknesses became less mutually
off-limits; our trust thinned, and turned, almost, to distaste.
Our friendship began to feel like too close weather,
impeding airflow and easy breathing.

I haven't collapsed from the freight of my late affection,
or from affection's absence in my sometime friend.
Perhaps, after all, we weren't a great match.
Yet, here I am, with all my tired furniture, reviewing
what seemed like connecting—and being revived.

Green

An old woman tries on
green glint earrings at a mall,
stream-green fluorite, frog-green jade,
malachite, like green shade. And green thoughts
flicker of her afternoons with a girlhood pal
who led her through dusty doors
of shops in Greenwich Village—
gleaming within like split geodes
with artful baubles for their ears and wrists—
and whose lithe black-tights-clad legs
and leaps in modern dance she wished
were hers, back in their wannabe Beatnik
salad days, and whose clandestine adventures
with boys, hinted in whispers
on those Village jaunts, were a primer
of glamour to come.

The many years of their
separate lives have drifted
down like dry brown leaves.
The old woman's letter,
written two decades ago,
trying to spark the flint
of their friendship, fell
into silence.

But inside memory's cracked rock—
as she puts the earrings back—
as if seen moments ago, and unchanged:
her friend's starkly white
face, framed in raven hair,
and her startling, pale green,
crystalline, chrysoprase eyes.

The Old Story Never Loses Its Capacity to Shock

Yesterday, the huge laugh spilling
from his throat, glorious,
at someone's joke, and everyone's pleasure
re-doubled by the raucousness. Yesterday,
triple-cream Brie, lavishly slathered
on chunks of baguette, luxurious
on his tongue, devoured
with such appetite, chased
by a generous swallow
of champagne.
Today, after the call,
the molecules of air
no longer effervesce.

How still it is.

Strange

Another loved one sentenced
to death by cancer—the door
to morning rooms and long, lazy
awakenings watching dust dance
in shafts of sun, slammed
in her face. And though
we'll all be shut out of the light later,
or sooner, it's always so strange
when we first hear. As if this world
were our eternal birthright,
the sweet trivial decisions—
sourdough or wheat,
decaf or tea—ours to make
forever.

When my turn comes, through the violence
of returning illness,
or in the labyrinth of sleep,
and I'm a shade—if shades can miss—
I think I'd miss these morning moments
ordinary as grass the most:
how we emerged from the shadowed
forests of the night
into the sunny meadow
of the gifted day—
bread becoming golden
in the toaster, sending out
rivulets of fragrance, you
reading something funny
to me from the paper.

I Don't Think We Live in California

We drove down from grey inland,
for the first time in two pandemic years,
and now sit in our cover-up clothes
that ward off dangerous sun, like foreigners,
or anthropologists, or like a couple
of old codgers—wait, omit "like"—
on a bench overlooking a strip
of beach in Laguna. The sun
blinks behind clouds, then emerges,
the star of the afternoon. The mixture
of breeze and warmth exhilarates,
though we don't move. When
did thong bikini bottoms become
a thing? The young female bodies
in front of us playing beach
volleyball seem almost pre-
pubescently thin, as if built
for only the most parsimonious
of coverings. The walkers stream by—
the women jiggling like jello
in their midriff-baring bandeaux,
or à la mode in breezy pastel linen
elegant against bronzed skin.

Later, we wander into a Native American
jewelry shop, and find ourselves sharing
our similar views on Israel/Palestine
with the Palestinian owner. We are charmed,
and charming, I think, though he tells us
he took us for "out-of-state . . . *farmers*"
when we first walked in. He almost,
but doesn't say *hicks*.

Explosion

Decades together, yet still
white phosphorus in our chests.
Who strikes first? Does it matter?
We are each tinder.

A word misread as a missile
on either's radar—
and bombers rip
placid skies.

Afterwards, scorched, exhausted,
we both dig in and stoke the embers
in private underground shelters
flanking the de facto DMZ.

But we grow chilled and forlorn,
and crawl out of
our cellars, and creep back
across the landscape
we've laid waste

to lie, wordless, in each other's
arms—as if just awakening
from the same shocking nightmare,
in the only place of safety
and warmth.

Theft

My burning hip,
your aching neck,
my creaky knee,
your tender spine.

Now we sleep,
avoiding pain,
at outposts
of our spacious bed—
each wrapped in ancient
loneliness.

Once we drowsed
curled close as pups, your arm
clasped tight around
my waist, or face-
to-face, breathing
each other's breath.

Bodily Pain

sways over his beer
in a bar. Familiar, presumptuous,
he tells the same story over and over
with slurred conviction. It's fresh to him:
scandalous, astonishing,
augural. He's a proselytizer
for a church of one. Back and forth
he rocks like a lonely
bell, tolling, tolling, on an island
in the middle of the ocean.

8th and 9th Decade

She hears him, at last, at the door,
entering with the two dogs
after a long walk, hanging up
the leashes, coming down the hall,
and leaves the bedroom where
she's been dressing for their dinner
with a friend, to see blood rivering
over his face, *oh my God*—and hear
some story about how he lost his
center of gravity as he came downhill,
how he crumpled to the pavement,
head hitting last, with a discernible
thunk. She takes him into the bathroom,
makes him sit, and he lets her
wash and wash his forehead and cheeks until
she can see the abrasions, though they quibble
a bit about the choice of bandages,
until the extra large ones she insists on—
left over from some previous untoward
occasion—seem to perfectly fit.
He studies his eyes in the mirror—
they don't appear unequally dilated—wasn't that
a symptom of concussion? And off they go
to the chosen restaurant, where, after an hour
wait, they realize they have the wrong date.
That night, as they prepare for bed,
her nose-blowing leads to a deluge of glaring red
(*Those blood thinners, again!*)
that runs onto her mouth and over her clothes
and gathers thickly in her throat, but she can't
risk leaning over the sink to spit it out,
and is near panic until he sits her down,
tells her to count, slowly, to ten, hands her
pieces of cotton wool to stuff in her nostril.
She might think: *so this is how
our lives begin to come undone.* But
what she thinks is: *Oh my God we're so lucky.*

Escape

Sunday after Christmas in SoCal, and the mall
is crowded as Mecca, the mob
circumambulating the food court and then
clockwise, back. Fresh-faced schoolgirls,
bustier'd and booted, proud of the tattooed
masculine muscle slung around their plump
shoulders; women rippling in their tights stretching
their last gift dollars at many-pawed cut-price racks;
and me, in post-parties anomie,
flung along in what-did-I-come-for
confusion, hoping for cheer
but ending up feeling anything bought—
the stackable bangles weakly flashing their charms,
the gold-tone rope chain—while good for the lackluster
retail economy, would be goods
for the grave. Oh, I think I was trying to bury
the story fixed in my mind
of a friend's widowed mother only twenty years
older, gasping for breath through the long hours
of her death—the gift she most sought denied
by a cruel hospice doc
sanctifying the letter of the law—
though everyone had gathered
as if for a Christmas Eve party, though
she'd whispered *I'm ready.*

I ran to my car to get out of there,
out of here, of the fear, home to you
and some tea, and my book, and our bed,
and the radiant, holy, priceless dream
of waking beside you on infinite days.

Touch

What if, in my papery skin,
I am disappeared into one
of so many duplicate, remote
and solitary rooms—
quiet as the cells of abandoned
wasps' nests, or beehives?

What if I roll
to the floor in my sleep,
and there is only the squeeze
of the blood-pressure cuff, the cold coin
of the stethoscope on my chest?

What if, when my busy children
clear an hour to visit, they hug
their brittle progenitor
at a distance, like palms
arcing over in a wind?

What if I sit
with their gift of a robo-kitty
in my lap, and stroke
and stroke its back,
and coo in answer
to the answering mewing
and VibraPurring, and stroke
until the kitty rolls over
for a belly-rub—the warmth
of my own undiminished affections
flooding me—
and stroke until it
closes its glassy eyes and snoozes,
as I do?

Incommensurate

In the living world, the husband in his thin
robe, his floppy slippers, takes
the trash out to the street at dawn,
and collapses on the driveway.
The wife, drowsing in bed, warm,
expects him at her side, any minute.
The rising sun sends smoky rays
through the trees on the forest trail
they walked two days before,
while he lies still, impervious
to the concrete's cold.
The grandkids sleep deeply
in their bedroom across town,
after yesterday's blissed-out afternoon
digging at the beach
with their grandfolks-gifted shovels
and rakes, molds and pails.
The leaves of tall stalks of corn
in someone's kitchen garden rustle
in a mild breeze. In the wife's daybreak
dream, she stands on the shore
of a lake the couple never planned
to visit, whose water is always black, even
at midday. She will not
go in. He already has.

If I Could Use the Wind Phone . . .

Inside [the phone box] there is an old black telephone, disconnected, that carries voices
into the wind . . . . [P]eople who have lost someone . . . pick up the receiver to speak to
the other side. —Literary Hub, March 17, 2021

I think I would feel shy with Mom and Dad, settled
for decades in their grey subterranean country,
wandering passageways in their no longer new
shapes permeable as vapor, whispering
in their no longer new language—fainter
than air brushing past my ears—
and faltering, now, in the language
we once shared.

It might be easier to talk with my brother-in-law,
only three years gone, to finally return
his generous weekly calls inquiring after each
of the members of his brother's nuclear family,
even the dogs. Perhaps I could be
hearty with him, as if he were in for a brief
hospital stay, and coming home soon.
But my questions would stick in my throat,
as they do when I think of my uncles
and aunts, my sister-in-law, my cousins
and friends—all dispersed on the wind:
Are you sleeping comfortably?
Are you able to eat?

Those who manage to use the wind phone
must talk the way I talk to our living dogs,
patting myself with words as I move
through my day on those rare occasions
when you, my love, have traveled far from home . . .
For my lunch—tuna on sourdough? Or cheese
and tomato? Chime in, guys.

But, if you depart to Forever
before me, and silence buzzes
like static in my ears, and the house fills
with a viscous invisible fog
I self-consciously push through,
preternaturally alone—
your absolute Absence
will make all words withdraw.

Anticipation

In the dawn chill, in the too-quiet
late afternoon, separation waits.
I will rush from our bed or my desk
to find you first—working the crossword
at the breakfast table, or pulling dandelions
in the yard as the light fails. I will wrap myself
to you close as gauze to heal the inescapable
rift—make us two birds fellable
with one stone.

Final Dissolve by Aquamation

If only there were stations of the air like the flamboyant clouds
in Baroque paintings, around which putti peek
in dizzying vistas, and—necks craned back—
we could count out the platforms of our apotheoses—
turning rose-gold in the setting sun . . .

If there were ladders like Jacob's, each rung
festooned with bluebells and fuchsia
like something out of Fragonard, each step
a light bounce upward easy as the breeze,
as a chorus of countertenor angels sings . . .

But no. Bitter as a slap against the cheek by the hand
of someone adored—that last crossover at first impossible
to absorb: from spirit—our beloved's animated
face, her moving hands, her joys—to 2%
of her original weight in white ash.

The Dead

We say may their memories be
for a blessing, we invoke their names
many times as the years circle,
always ending at a new place,
like a spiral, we ask God
to remember our ancestors
and their merit when we pray
for ourselves. But they
fade. Even our images of them
walk away from us,
dimming like the plots of once-loved
books, until they are less, and more—
an almost recognizable ray
of sun touching our shoulders
on a chill day of alternating brightness
and drizzle, the kindness of the first
lamps switched on in the smoke-blue dusk.

Deep Travel

I was a child in a five-boroughed Garden of Eden/city—
the given, new, and crumbling, shining, grimy
world. And I heard talk of "sixth boroughs,"
places with the thickness of familiarity, places I imagined
I could pass into with no resistance—the way ghosts passed
through walls in 50s TV fantasies—and be at home.
And now so many once-strange latitudes have addresses in my mind,
which light up warmly when I hear or read their names: 7th, 8th, 9th,
10th, 11th "boroughs," so different from the 1st through 6th,
yet naturalized in the *longue durée* of cumulative or extended visits.

Sometimes there's a kind of placeless favorite weather in my dreams,
jacket-cool as June in Norway, or autumn in the little park not far
from our Bronx apartment—light glancing, breeze-tossed, in the trees—
and I don't know where I am. Or there's a rhythmic brilliance
of magenta, flame, and lavender, that could be the joyous spring decor
in lamppost flowerpots in almost any town in France, or my long-gone
aunt's hanging baskets down-dripping with impatiens in her summer
garden in Roslyn, Long Island. Sometimes I savor a sense
of restful busyness in whatever task I'm carrying out—
like the calm of Fanti fishermen mending their nets
on the Ghanaian coast, their smooth backs gleaming in the sun.
Sometimes my loneliness feels summed by a solitary red
farmhouse casting its shadow on the snow—on a spit of land
jutting into a fjord, or on the great plains of North Dakota.

Some part of me yet hopes, when I'm poled across
that last black frothing river, I will disembark
with no resistance, and be welcome
in the final borough, the 12th, perhaps.

Afternoon, Evening, Night

i

On the closed blinds covering
my study's west-facing windows—
as if they were a translucent
rice paper screen—shadows
of a few outside leaves
lift and sway, stirring
in a soundless wind.
Now they become agitated.
Now becalmed. Then they are
flustered again.

A flare of light brightens
the edge of a cushion.
Like a guttering candle,
a flush of light
flickers on my dulling page.

Soon, as if the trees outside
have walked closer, quiet leaf-shadow
almost fills the double windows.

In a little while,
the warm flutters in the room
are quenched. And then,
the closed blinds turn flat gray—
the shadow play is over.

ii

First there was darkness,
over the face of Ocean,
and then the Splendor!

But light did not expunge
the dark.

It comes now
slowly down.
It hushes the streets outside
the shuttered windows of my town.

It settles like a quilted
throw a daughter places
over the old woman
fallen asleep in her chair.

Its kind wing mantles
towns and fields,
towns and fields,
towns and fields,
until it dims your town
and your street,
and then, the mountains,
and the sea.

Cosmoses

Curled in my college carrel, I loved to read
about the spinning crystalline spheres, made
of the fifth element, mysterious and pure—
like the planets they carried—and all cozily tucked
inside each other, humming as if struck
by God's tuning fork. Back then, I learned,
the central Earth was the stagnant
pit—though firmly in the regard of God—
where all four elements warred, as they warred
in man, pinnacle of created beings, possessed
of a rational soul, yet easily dragged
to hell, just underneath his feet.

I loved how The Book of Nature's "soulless" beasts—
companionably allegorical, neatly accordant
with the Book of God—pranced, crawled,
and slithered across cathedral walls, stained-glass
windows and the pages of illuminated manuscripts.

It all seemed as holdable in my mind
as a snow globe in my hand, and easy to expound
on tests, compared to the cosmos we occupy now,
impossible to wrap my head around, and—according
to "the principle of mediocrity"—nowhere special:
all the same.

What would the ancient readers
of those congruent Books make of Evolution's
endless, chance-engendered creativity
extending to the "lowest" species:
single-cell slime with memory, if not a mind;
flies extruding glue from their feet to walk
on ceilings; ants with a seating plan for rafts
of themselves that float out of disaster?
(While we, so "noble in reason," keep flunking
stewardship of nature.)

What would those readers, what can I
make of this universe measurable only
in exponential trails of zeros, this universe
that could wink out (since it winked on)—long after
the charred Earth is gobbled by the Sun,
no privileged humans having previously come
to tell of their exempted ascensions
into a pure and eternal Empyrean?
What can I do inside this dizzying, perishable
immensity, but live in astonishment
that we are here at all, however briefly?

Judy Kronenfeld's six full-length books of poetry include *Groaning and Singing* (FutureCycle, 2022), *Bird Flying through the Banquet* (FutureCycle, 2017) and *Shimmer* (WordTech, 2012). Her poems have appeared in four dozen anthologies and in many journals including *Cider Press Review, Gyroscope Review, MacQueen's Quinterly, New Ohio Review, One Art, Rattle, Sheila-Na-Gig, Valparaiso Poetry Review* and *Verdad*. Judy has also published criticism—including *King Lear and the Naked Truth* (Duke, 1998)—short stories, and creative nonfiction. Her third chapbook, *Oh Memory, You Unlocked Cabinet of Amazements!*, is forthcoming from Bamboo Dart in June, 2024, and her memoir-in-essays, *Apartness*, from Inlandia Books in 2024/2025.

Sheila-Na-Gig Editions